# Having Fun
# In Grandma's Day

by Valerie Weber
and Valerie Jane McNamara

✦ Carolrhoda Books, Inc./Minneapolis

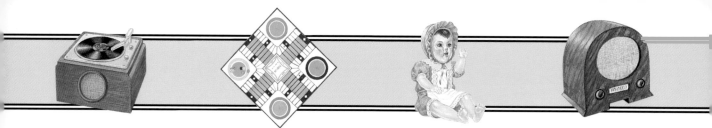

Carolrhoda Books, Inc., A Division of the Lerner Publishing Group
241 First Avenue North, Minneapolis, MN 55401 U.S.A.

Website address: www.lernerbooks.com

Planning and production by Discovery Books
Edited by Faye Gardner
Text designed by Ian Winton
Illustrations by Stuart Lafford
Commissioned photography by Sabine Beaupré and Jim Wend

The publishers would like to thank Valerie Jane McNamara for her help in the preparation of this book.

Library of Congress Cataloging-in-Publication Data

Weber, Valerie.
   Having fun in grandma's day / by Valerie Weber and Valerie Jane McNamara.
      p.   cm. — (In grandma's day)
   Includes index.
   Summary: An account, focusing on the leisure time activities, of the life of Valerie Jane McNamara, who grew up in the Midwest during the 1940s.
   ISBN 1-57505-325-X
   1. Middle West—Social life and customs—Juvenile literature.   2. McNamara, Valerie Jane—Childhood and youth—Juvenile literature.   3. Middle West—Biography—Juvenile literature.   [1. Middle West—Social life and customs.   2. McNamara, Valerie Jane—Childhood and youth.   3. Women—Biography.]   I. McNamara, Valerie Jane.   II. Title.   III. Series: Weber, Valerie.  In grandma's day.
F354.W43   1999
956—dc21                                                    98-5500

Printed in Hong Kong
Bound in the United States of America
1 2 3 4 5 6 - OS - 04 03 02 01 00 99

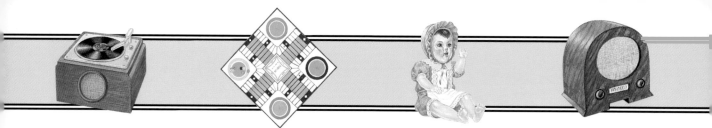

# Contents

# A Growing Family

Hi! I'm Valerie Jane McNamara. I have nine grandchildren, ranging in age from two to eighteen years old. Here I am with two of my grandchildren, Dan, who is sixteen, and Greg, who is twelve. The other photo shows three more of my grandchildren, Chris, who is eight, Connor, who is five, and Clare, who is three.

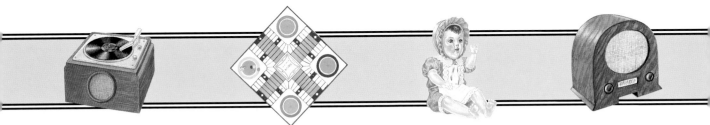

I was born in 1935 and grew up in Milwaukee, Wisconsin. My dad was a businessman, and my mother worked at home. My father was Polish, and my mother was German.

This family photo was taken when I was almost eleven years old. I'm standing in front of my dad, and my big sister, Marilyn, is next to me holding our baby sister, Deirdre. Marilyn is four years older than me. We had lots of fun growing up together.

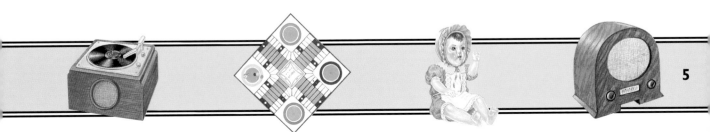

# Entertaining Ourselves

Some of our games might be different from the ones you play. Few people had heard of computers, televisions were scarce, and the VCR was not even dreamed of. We entertained ourselves in so many different ways in the 1940s. Sometimes we dressed up and put on little shows, mostly just for ourselves. My parents liked to come and watch.

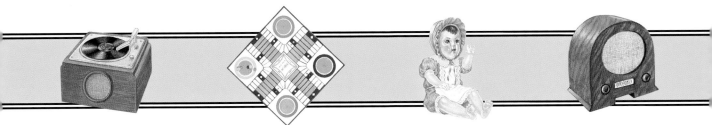

I loved going to my relatives' houses to make music. My uncles and cousins played many different instruments, and we liked to sing around the piano.

Our favorite songs were "The Band Played On," "Beautiful Ohio," and anything by the Andrews Sisters, a popular singing group of the time. The Andrews Sisters are shown in the photograph above.

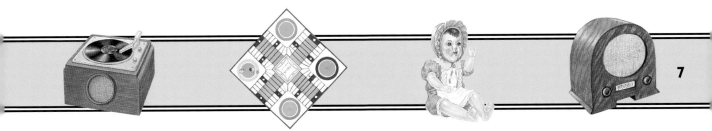

## Radio Fun

In the 1940s, television was still pretty new. I only saw TVs in stores. It seemed like all those televisions ever showed was boxing! Hardly anyone owned a TV set. We did have a big wooden radio that stood on the floor. It looked like the radio in this photograph.

I loved listening to the radio. Sometimes when my mom and dad went out to the movies, my mom would make candy for my sister and me. My sister and I would crawl under the dining room table and listen to our favorite shows, mysteries like *The Shadow, Suspense Theater,* and *Inner Sanctum.* I loved those scary shows.

I also liked *Tom Mix*, a cowboy show on the radio. There were Tom Mix movies, too. I remember sending away for a special Tom Mix ring that glowed in the dark. We waited for weeks to get that in the mail.

Music was different, too. We listened to ballads, love songs, and waltzes on the radio and the record player. No one had even thought of rock and roll, and rhythm and blues was seldom heard on the radio. I loved songs like "That Old Black Magic" and "As Time Goes By," but my favorite was "You'll Never Know," sung by Alice Faye. I could imagine myself being a famous singer singing that song.

Like most families in the 1940s, we didn't have many toys, but we sure had fun. My favorite toy was a doll. I liked to rock my doll in a cradle attached to my rocking chair. I would sing to her and put her to bed.

At that time, some schools let students borrow a toy from school. I was always happy to get something new to play with for a week. Sometimes I'd choose a doll, and other times I would bring home a high chair or a doll buggy.

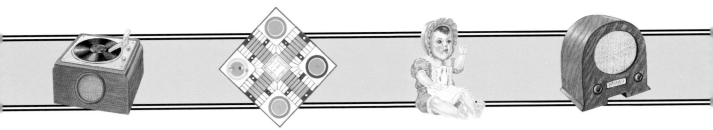

I had my own friends, but I played a lot with my older sister. Marilyn and I made dolls out of wooden clothespins to use in our puppet theater. Sometimes we played with paper doll cutouts.

You might play some of the games we liked, such as Monopoly. I also loved playing hopscotch. We drew squares on the

sidewalk in colored chalk. Then we threw a stone onto each square, one at a time, and tried to jump on each of the other squares without touching the chalk lines. I liked jumping rope, too. When I was twelve, I learned how to jump double Dutch, with two ropes twirling at the same time.

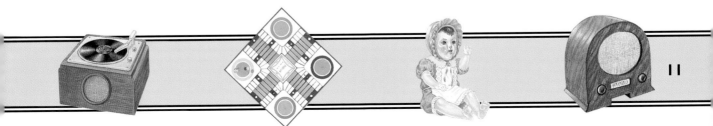

## Playing with Friends

When I was six, we lived in a house with fields in the back. Sometimes we made bonfires from piles of leaves and roasted apples and marshmallows.

The sweet smell drew friends from the neighborhood to play. Here I am with my mom in our yard.

My friends and I often made up our own games. We pretended we were movie stars and acted out scenes or sang songs from our favorite movies. Sometimes the boys played, too, but they preferred action movies like *Tarzan* or stories from comics like the *Adventure* series.

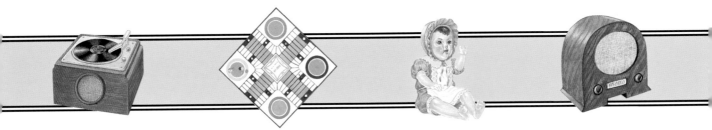

We played baseball in the field behind the house or Kick the Can in the street. In Kick the Can, we set a soup can in the middle of the street and kicked it as far as we could.

While everyone ran and hid, the person chosen to be "It" put the can back. Then It looked for the rest of us, hoping to find someone before we could kick the can

again. If It found someone, he or she would yell that person's name and run as fast as possible back to the can. If the hidden person beat It back to the can, It had to keep on searching.

Kick the Can was an exciting game, especially when we played it right before it got dark outside. Sometimes it took me a while to hear my mother calling me in to go to bed.

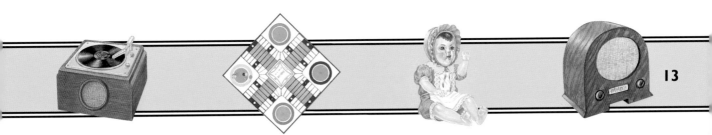

# Trading Cards and Streetcars

At school during recess, Renee Fleishmann, who was my best friend, and I brought out our shoeboxes full of trading cards. The cards had different pictures on them. We collected cards with pictures of cats, dogs, and gardens.

But the best cards were pictures of pretty girls in different costumes, who were known as Petty girls. I tried to get as many of those as possible.

After school, Renee and I liked to play near the electric streetcars. We would put a flat stone on a rail and watch as a streetcar came along and ran over it, shattering the stone into tiny pieces. We were always relieved we hadn't made the streetcar tip over and hurt the passengers. Even though this could have been a dangerous game, we played it again and again.

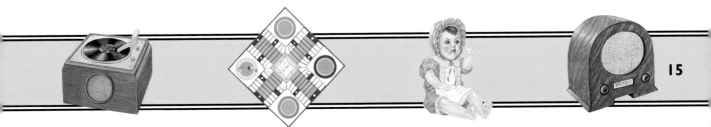

## Reading for Fun

After school ended in the summer, I would join the Bookworm Club at the local library.

Each time I finished a book, the librarian stamped my paper with a little worm with a face on it. I was very proud when I filled up my sheet with worm stamps.

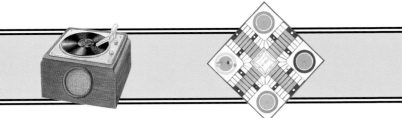

I loved biographies, especially stories of explorers and woodsmen like Kit Carson and Davy Crockett, and mysteries, like Nancy Drew.

One of my favorite books was *The Road to Oz*. I read it over and over!

I liked to curl up in the living room with my dog next to me and read.

## Going to the Movies

From 1941 until 1945, the United States fought in World War II in Europe and in Asia, including Japan. Many families had someone — a husband, a son, or a daughter — in the armed forces. My cousin Ralph was in Italy, repairing trucks for the army.

I remember walking to the movies with my mother and seeing stars in the windows of the houses we passed. A blue star meant that the family had someone in the war. A gold star meant that a family member had died in the war. That always made me very sad.

The movies helped cheer me up again. The theaters were much larger then, and we could see two movies at a time, one after another.  My favorite theaters were named the Mars, the Grand, and the Hollywood.

The dwarfs sing their marching song on the way to work.

Ushers would show us to our seats, shining a flashlight so we could see in the dark.  Until I was twelve, I only had to pay twelve cents to see a movie.

## Serials and Popcorn

We saw dramatic movies like *Mrs. Miniver* and comedies like *The Dolly Sisters*. I liked anything to do with movie stars because I wanted to be a star, too.

I also liked the shows called serials, such as *Superman*. Serials were stories divided into episodes. Movie theaters showed them at Saturday matinees, or afternoon shows. Each episode ended with an exciting scene that made us want to come back the next week to see what happened. A serial could last ten weeks. I hated missing even one episode.

Based on the SUPERMAN adventure feature appearing in SUPERMAN and ACTION COMICS magazines, in daily and Sunday newspapers coast-to-coast and on the SUPERMAN radio program broadcast over the Mutual Network.

with
**SUPERMAN**
KIRK  NOEL  TOMMY  CAROL
**ALYN·NEILL·BOND·FORMAN**

Adaptation by
GEORGE H. PLYMPTON and JOSEPH F. POLAND

Chapter 3
The REDUCER RAY

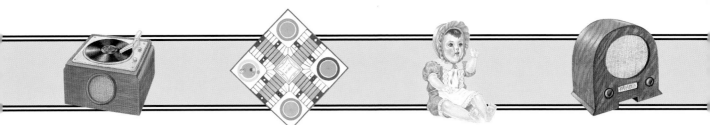

For ten cents, we got a bag of popcorn that my whole family shared. When I was eleven, Marilyn had a boyfriend who always bought me a bag of popcorn when I went to the movies with them. I had the whole bag to myself!

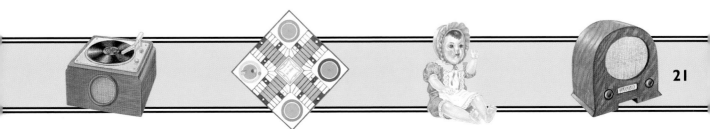

## Christmas

Holidays were the times when we had the most fun of all. At Christmastime, I would rush home from Girl Scout meetings to listen to Billie the Brownie on the radio. He was an elf who read letters that children had sent to Santa. He made me dream about Christmas Eve and the presents I wanted. It was always hard to wait.

You can see Billie the Brownie in this picture. He is the elf on the left.

My family always went to church after dinner on Christmas Eve. When we got home, my sisters and I would go into a bed-room to wait for Santa. It was so exciting to hear the sounds of

Santa in the next room. His bells would jingle as he called out good-bye. Then my parents would let us into the living room to see the presents under the tree shining with tinsel. I remember one year I got a doll, a doll buggy, and a cradle. My mom made clothes for the doll and blankets for the cradle.

## Fourth of July Celebrations

Other holidays could be just as special.  Our Fourth of July celebration might have been similar to yours.  Every year, I would decorate my baby buggy and march in the Fourth of July parade, hoping to win a prize.  Once I dressed up my china baby doll and put her in the buggy, too.  I was so happy when I finally won second prize—a game.

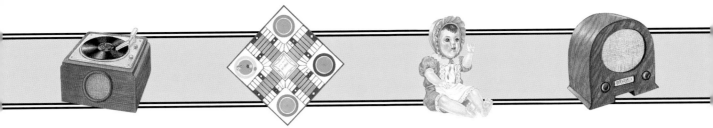

At the Fourth of July picnic later in the day, everyone got an ice-cream cup. Inside the lid, under a thin sheet of paper, were pictures of movie stars like Greer Garson or Humphrey Bogart. Marilyn and I saved them and put them on our bedroom walls.

The mayor might come and sing songs at the picnic, especially "John Brown's Baby." The crowd sang

along. At night, we gathered on blankets in the park along the shores of Lake Michigan, thrilled by the fireworks lighting up the sky.

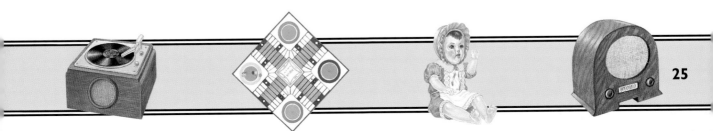

# Birthday Fun

My birthday was very important to me. I remember when my mother was baking a cake for my seventh birthday and the air-raid sirens went off. The sirens meant that we were having an air-raid drill.

During an air-raid drill, we practiced what we would do if enemy airplanes flew over us. We had to turn off all the lights so the enemy couldn't see where our town was. Air-raid wardens wearing helmets walked every neighborhood, making sure everyone followed the drill rules.

During this air-raid drill, the electricity went off, so off went the lights and the oven with my cake baking in it! My mother was so mad. But the cake turned out all right.

# The Best Celebration of All

There was one celebration I'll never forget. In the summer of 1945, my sister and I were on our way to camp when the news came that the Japanese had surrendered, or quit fighting. The war was over! All around us, people were laughing, hugging, ringing bells, and even crying because they were so happy.

We didn't get to see the big celebrations that week, but we enjoyed life at camp with all the crafts, horseback riding, and swimming. When I got home, my dad gave me a poster like this one to keep as a souvenir of the victory celebrations. We'd made it through wartime and even had some fun along the way.

# Glossary

**air-raid:** an attack by a military airplane, usually one that drops bombs. During World War II, the mainland of the United States was never bombed. Communities held air-raid drills, practices in case of attack, so that people would know what to do if their community was ever bombed.

**episode:** one part of a movie or television show that is shown in many parts

**matinee:** an afternoon showing of a movie or a performance

**serial:** a long story broken up into parts

**streetcar:** a vehicle for carrying people, powered by electric wires strung along a street. Unlike a bus, a streetcar runs along tracks set in the middle of a city street.

**trading cards:** small cards, with a picture on the front and information on the back, that people collect and trade

Duden, Jane. *Timeline: 1940s.* New York: Crestwood House, 1989.

Evert, Jodi, editor. *Molly's Craft Book: A Look at Crafts from the Past with Projects You Can Make Today.* Middleton, Wisc.: Pleasant Company Publications, Inc., 1994

Galt, Margot Fortunato. *Up to the Plate: The All American Girls Professional Baseball League.* Minneapolis, Minn.: Lerner Publications Co., 1995.

McClary, Andrew. *Toys with Nine Lives: A Social History of American Toys.* North Haven, Conn.: Linnet Books, 1997.

Rubel, David. *The United States in the 20th Century.* New York: Scholastic, Inc., 1995.

Whitman, Sylvia. *V Is for Victory: The American Homefront during World War II.* Minneapolis, Minn.: Lerner Publications Co., 1993.

# Index